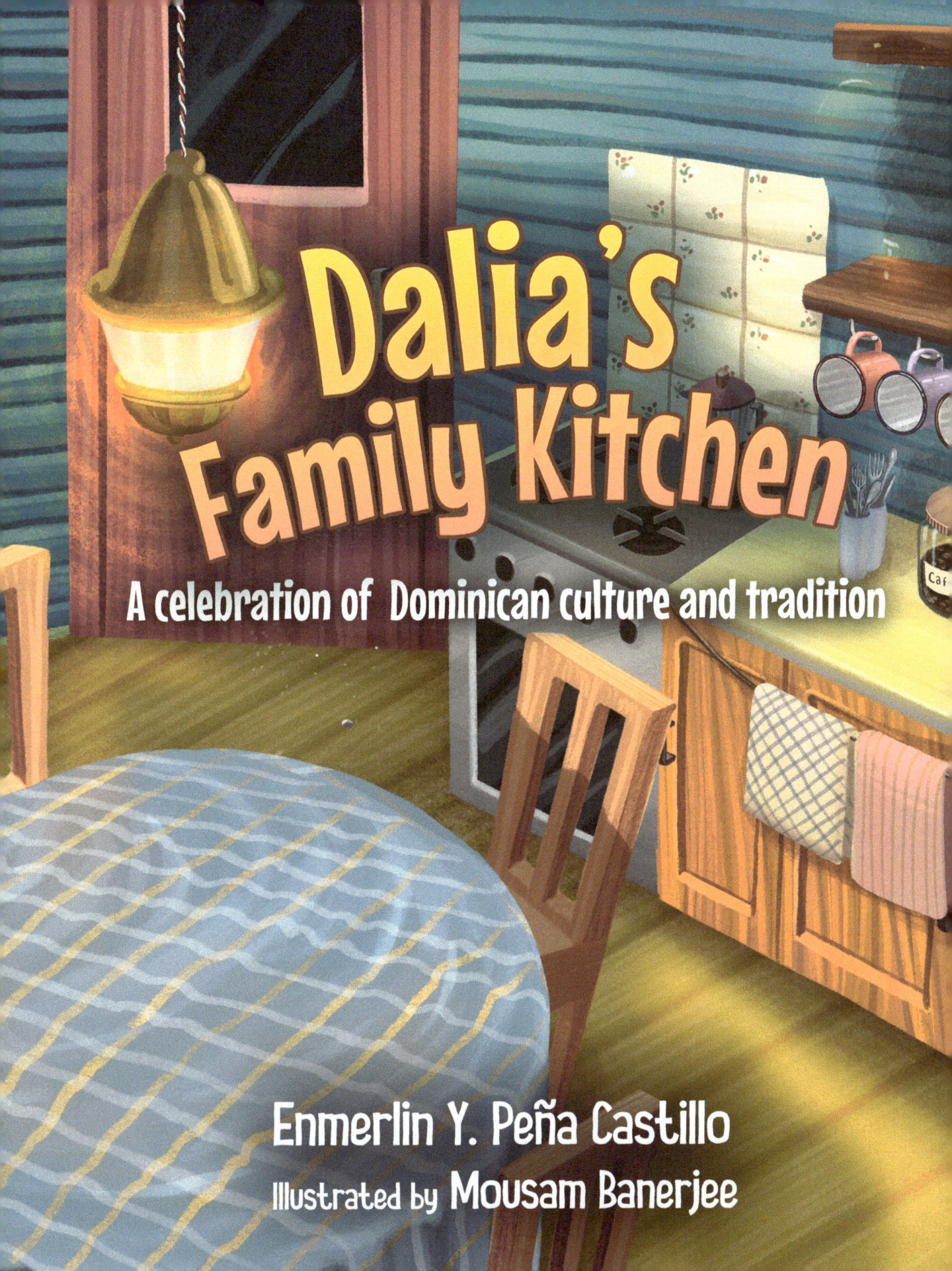

Copyright © 2025 Enmerlin Y. Peña Castillo

All rights reserved. No part of this book may be reproduced, distributed, or transmitted in any form or by any means, electronic or mechanical, including photocopying, recording, or any information storage and retrieval system, without the prior written permission of the author, except for brief quotations used in critical articles or reviews.
Thank you for purchasing an authorized edition of this book. By complying with copyright laws, you help protect the creative work of authors and artists. Please refrain from reproducing, scanning, or distributing any part of this book in any form without express permission.
Written by: Enmerlin Y. Peña Castillo
Illustrated by: Mousam Banerjee
ISBN: 979-8-9995474-1-5

This book is dedicated to my beloved grandparents, Dilia and Carmito, who not only taught me the art of cooking but also revealed the profound power of a home-cooked meal to bring people together, forge lasting bonds, and celebrate our shared heritage. Every dish I prepare feels like a journey back in time, to my childhood home, wrapped in the warmth of their embrace. I am forever grateful for the wisdom they passed down to me, especially their deep reverence for the abundance of our land and the importance of honoring those who cultivate it to nourish our community. Their love, lessons, and legacy live on in every meal I make.

She lived in a modest wood house near the river. Dalia loved spending time in her family's kitchen. This kitchen was a magical land where colorful fruits, fresh vegetables, and fragrant herbs unlocked her creativity and inspired her imagination.

Dalia's greatest inspiration was her grandmother, Mamá Carmen.

Mamá Carmen taught Dalia the secret family recipes passed down through generations, each one a treasure trove of flavors honoring their ancestors and their Dominican heritage.

One day, Dalia decided it was time to share her cooking talent and delicious family recipes with the children from her village.

Filled with joy, she invited all the children from the village to her kitchen for a special cooking class.

Excitement and curiosity filled the kitchen as all the children gathered around Dalia, eager to learn.

With Mamá Carmen by her side, Dalia taught the children how to make tostones, using only the freshest green plantains from the garden and a sprinkle of sea salt.

The children smiled with delight as they enjoyed the crispy, flavorful golden-brown tostones.

Next, Dalia showed them how to make mangú, served with savory cheese, crispy salami, and perfectly round fried eggs.

The children were filled with joy and gratitude. They lifted their sticky hands while laughing and dancing around the kitchen after mashing the plantains together.

As the sun went to sleep, Dalia surprised her guests with a grand feast. Together, they sat around the table, sharing stories and laughter as they savored juicy chicken, crispy tostones, and sweet arroz con leche.

From that day on, Dalia's kitchen became a place of joy, community, and wonder for the whole village.

Children would gather to learn the magic of cooking with love and honoring their heritage through nutritious and delicious meals.

And so, Dalia's culinary adventures continued, spreading love, laughter, and the rich flavors of the Dominican Republic wherever she went.

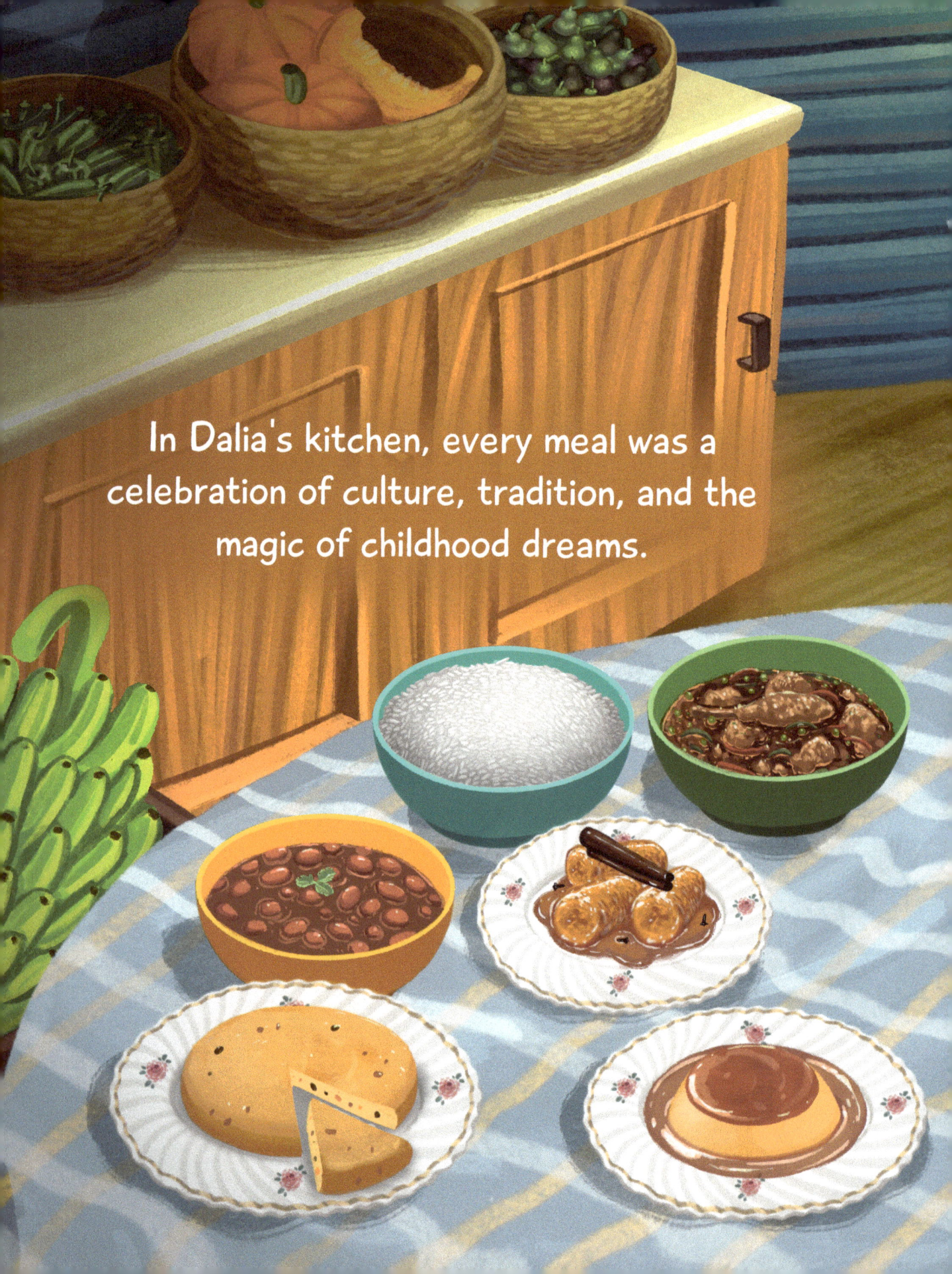

In Dalia's kitchen, every meal was a celebration of culture, tradition, and the magic of childhood dreams.

# Reading Comprehension Questions

1. What does Dalia teach the children to make first?

2. Who is Dalia's biggest inspiration in the kitchen?

3. What is mangú served with in the story?

4. How do the children react after tasting the tostones?

5. What does the kitchen symbolize for the village children by the end of the story?

6. Which of Dalia's recipes would you like to try making at home?

# Family Recipes

Thank you for exploring Dominican culture through our story, our love for sharing home-cooked meals, and the family recipes that connect us to our roots. Cooking is a labor of love. We believe food has the power to bring family, friends, and neighbors together to build a stronger, more caring community where everyone feels welcome. Cooking is a beautiful and soulful art, and like any artistic endeavor, the cook should always feel free to add their own special touch to every dish.

# Origins of Dominican Cuisine

Dominican cuisine is influenced by Indigenous Taíno, African, and Spanish culinary traditions.

The Indigenous Taíno people, who inhabited the island before European colonization, contributed greatly to Dominican gastronomy. They cultivated cassava (yuca), sweet potatoes, maíz (corn), and various fruits, which remain central to Dominican dishes. They also developed cooking methods such as steaming in leaves.

During the colonial period, the Spanish brought enslaved Africans to the island. Along with their labor, Africans introduced many ingredients, cooking techniques, and flavor profiles that became integral to Dominican cuisine. Key contributions include the use of plantains, rice, and beans, as well as the practice of frying foods. African cooking styles also influenced the preparation of stews and the use of seasonings.

The Spanish brought their own culinary traditions, including meats like pork, beef, and chicken, along with techniques such as roasting and frying. They introduced spices like garlic, onion, and saffron, which are still commonly used in Dominican cooking today.

Over time, the fusion of these three cultures resulted in what we know today as Dominican cuisine.

References: Hostelería News. La cocina dominicana: origen y evolución. Confederación Panamericana de Escuelas de Hotelería, Gastronomía y Turismo (CONPEHT). Historia y Gastronomía, República Dominicana. Embajada de la República Dominicana en Japón. Gastronomía.

# Cooking and Safety Tips
(Here are some essential tips to help you cook delicious meals)

Cooking together is a fun and educational way for kids and parents to bond and learn new skills. Follow these tips to ensure a safe and enjoyable kitchen experience.

## For Kids:
1. Always cook with adult supervision.
2. Wash your hands before handling food.
3. Stick to kid-friendly tools and avoid sharp knives.
4. Stay away from stoves and ovens, and always use mitts for hot items.
5. Avoid distractions and focus on your culinary creation.

## For Parents:
1. Keep the kitchen clean and hazardous items out of reach.
2. Provide age-appropriate utensils and supervise their use.
3. Explain and demonstrate safe cooking practices.
4. Turn pot handles inward and keep them out of reach.
5. Ensure safe use of blenders and mixers.

# General tips to help you cook delicious meals:

1. Read the entire recipe before you start cooking to avoid unpleasant surprises.
2. Measure and prepare all your ingredients before you start cooking.
3. Season your food in layers.
4. Always taste your food, it will tell you what it needs.
5. Use heat in your favor. Use high heat for searing, medium heat for simmering, and low heat for gentle cooking.
6. When possible, use fresh ingredients.
7. Bring meat to room temperature before cooking and let it rest after cooking for a more flavorful and tender outcome.
8. Clean as you go.
9. You do not need fancy cookware.
10. Add your own twist.
11. Try again!

# Seasoning Blends

# Dry Herb Blend
(Mezcla de hierbas secas)

Preparation:

1. Combine all the herbs in a bowl and mix thoroughly. Store the blend in an airtight container for future use. This versatile herb mix is perfect for seasoning roasted vegetables, as well as white and red meats.

2. Enjoy!

4 tbsp dry oregano

4 tbsp dry thyme

4 tbsp dry parsley

4 tbsp dry basil

2 tbsp dry rosemary

# Wet Seasoning Blend

(The wet seasoning blend (sofrito) will be the utilized in both the chicken stew and red beans recipes)

Preparation:

1. Place all the ingredients in a food processor or blender and blend until smooth or until you reach your desired consistency. Store the mixture in an airtight container in the refrigerator, or freeze it for longer storage.

2. Enjoy!

# The Flag
(La bandera)

# White Rice
(Arroz blanco)

Preparation:

1. Rinse the rice 2 or 3 times with room temperature water, or until the water runs mostly clear. This step is optional and based on personal preference.

2. In a hot, deep pot, heat the olive oil and salt over medium heat for 25 to 35 seconds.

3. Add the rice to the pot and stir for about 1 minute. Then, pour in the water and cook over medium heat until it reduces by about 90%.

4. Reduce the heat to low and cover the pot tightly with foil. Place the lid on top to trap the moisture. Let it cook for 15 to 18 minutes.

5. Carefully remove the lid and gently stir the rice, avoiding scraping the bottom of the pot. Cover again and cook for an additional 10 to 15 minutes.

6. Serve and enjoy!

# Red Beans
(Habichuelas rojas)

Preparation:

1. Soak the beans overnight in 11 cups of water. The next day, add a small onion peeled and cut in half, 2 celery sticks cut in half, and 1 carrot to the beans. Boil over medium to high heat for 1 hour and 40 minutes, or until the beans are tender. Remove from heat.

2. For a pressure cooker, soak the beans overnight in 9 cups of water. Add a small onion peeled and cut in half, 2 celery sticks cut in half, and 1 carrot. Boil for 10 minutes, then pressure cook for 25 to 30 minutes, or until the beans are tender. Remove from heat.

3. Once cooked, take out the carrot, celery, and onion, along with 1 cup of beans. Blend these with 2 cups of water until smooth, then strain this mixture back into the pot to give the beans a creamier texture.

4. In a small frying pan, heat olive oil and add the wet seasoning blend, chicken bouillon, pepper, and tomato paste. Stir until the chicken bouillon dissolves and the tomato paste is well mixed. Add half a cup of bean cooking liquid, stir, and pour this mixture into the pot with the beans.

5. Return the pot to the stove over medium heat. Stir in salt, sugar, and vinegar. Boil for 5 to 7 minutes, taste, and adjust seasoning as needed.

6. Serve and enjoy!

# Chicken Stew
(Pollo guisado)

## Preparation:

1. Trim off any excess fat and cut the chicken into 3 to 4-inch pieces. Marinate it in sour orange juice for 3 to 5 minutes. If sour oranges aren't available, substitute with the juice of 2 limes. After marinating, rinse the chicken under cold water and pat dry.

2. In a large container, combine the chicken with sofrito, salt, pepper, and chicken bouillon. Stir thoroughly to ensure all pieces are evenly coated. Cover and refrigerate overnight for richer flavor.

3. Remove the marinated chicken from the refrigerator about 1 hour before cooking to let it come to room temperature.

4. In a deep-frying pan, heat olive oil over medium heat. Add 1 teaspoon of sugar and cook until it caramelizes (watch closely to avoid burning). Add the chicken pieces one at a time to the pan and sear for about 5 minutes on each side until lightly browned.

5. Pour 3 1/2 cups of water into the container that held the marinade and mix to capture any remaining seasoning. Add this liquid to the pan with the chicken. Bring to a boil over high heat. Taste and adjust salt as needed. Reduce heat to low, cover, and let it simmer for 1 hour and 15 minutes. Then increase the heat to medium-high and cook uncovered for an additional 10 minutes, or until the sauce thickens.

6. Serve and enjoy!

2 pounds chicken (24 oz)

1 chicken bouillon

2 sour oranges

1 tsp salt

1/4 tsp pepper

2/3 cup wet seasoning blend (sofrito)

2 tbsp olive oil

1/8 cup tomato paste

1 1/4 tsp white sugar

1/2 tsp vinegar

3 1/2 cups water

# Green Salad

(Ensalada verde)

Preparation:

1. Start by washing your vegetables thoroughly. In a bowl, combine the sliced beetroot with a sprinkle of white sugar, then cover and set aside. Slice the cucumber, tomato, and onion.

2. Arrange the romaine lettuce on a serving platter, ensuring it covers the entire platter, including the edges. In the center of the platter, place the shredded cabbage. Surround the cabbage with the sliced tomatoes, then layer the cucumber slices on top of each tomato slice. Next, add the beetroot slices on top of each cucumber slice. Finally, arrange the sliced onions around the platter.

3. For the dressing, mix the garlic, salt, and balsamic vinegar in a bowl, stirring until the salt dissolves. Add the oregano and mix well. Incorporate a splash of honey or agave, then stir until combined. Finish by adding the olive oil and mixing until the dressing is well blended.

4. Drizzle the dressing over the salad and enjoy!

# Fried Green Plantains

(Plátanos fritos o tostones)

Preparation:

1. Peel and slice the plantains into pieces about 1-inch thick.

2. Heat the oil in a deep-frying pan over medium heat. Fry the plantain slices for 1.5 to 2 minutes per side, being careful not to overcrowd the pan.

3. Remove the fried plantains and place them on a plate lined with paper towels to drain.

4. Once drained, flatten each plantain slice and return them to the pan. Fry for an additional 30 to 40 seconds per side, or until they are golden brown. Again, avoid overcrowding the pan.

5. Transfer the crispy plantains to a plate lined with paper towels and sprinkle with sea salt.

6. Serve and enjoy!

3 green plantains

1 1/2 cups frying oil

1/2 tsp sea salt

1/4 cup ketchup
(optional)

# Fried Sweet Plantains

(Plátanos maduros fritos)

Preparation:

1. Peel and slice the sweet plantains into pieces about 1-inch thick.

2. In a bowl, add the sliced sweet plantains, sprinkle the white sugar, and cover and set aside for 5 minutes.

3. Heat the oil in a deep-frying pan over medium heat. Fry the sweet plantain slices for about 2 minutes per side or until golden brown. Do not overcrowd the pan.

4. Transfer the fried sweet plantains to a serving plate and sprinkle with sea salt.

5. Serve and enjoy!

3 sweet plantains

1 1/2 cups frying oil

1/2 tsp white sugar

1/4 tsp sea salt

# Three Hits
(Tres golpes)

# Three Hits
(Tres golpes)

Preparation:

1. Start by peeling the plantains: cut off both ends, then make a slit along the side of each plantain and remove the peel. Place the peeled plantains in a pot with 4 cups of water and 1 tablespoon of salt. Boil over medium heat for 15-20 minutes or until the plantains are tender.

2. While the plantains cook, slice the onion into half-moon shapes and place them in a container with 1/4 cup of vinegar. Set aside to marinate.

3. Once the plantains are tender, drain them, reserving ½ cup of the cooking water. Mash the plantains using a potato masher, then add 1/4 cup of butter and a bit of the reserved water. For a smoother consistency, add 2-3 tablespoons of cold water while mashing. Set the mangú aside.

4. In a frying pan, heat 1/4 cup of neutral oil and fry the eggs to your desired consistency. Once the eggs are done, slice the salami into 1/3-inch wheels and fry them until golden brown on both sides. Next, slice the cheese into 1/3-inch rectangular pieces and fry them until golden on both sides.

5. Drain the marinated onions, but save the liquid. In a clean frying pan, heat 2 tablespoons of olive oil over medium heat. Add the onions and cook for 2-3 minutes. Pour in some of the reserved marinade and add a pinch of salt.

6. To serve, plate the mangú and top with the eggs, salami, and cheese. Use the sautéed onions as a garnish. Enjoy!

# Sweet Treats

# Rice Pudding

(Arroz con leche)

Preparation:

1. Rinse the rice with room temperature water 2 or 3 times, or until the water runs mostly clear. This step is optional and based on personal preference.

2. In a sauce pot, combine 1 cup of water with cloves, whole allspice, and 2 cinnamon sticks. Bring the mixture to a boil and let it simmer for 7 to 10 minutes, then remove from heat.

3. In a deep pot, strain the spice mixture, add the rice, water, whole milk, nutmeg, and 3 cinnamon sticks. Bring to a boil over medium heat and cook until the rice is tender.

4. Stir in the evaporated milk, coconut milk, condensed milk, vanilla extract, granulated sugar, salt, butter, and lime peel. Continue stirring until you reach your desired consistency. Keep in mind, when the rice cools down it will be thicker. Taste and adjust the sweetness and consistency as needed.

5. Serve and enjoy!

1 cup long grain white rice

1 cup evaporated milk

3 cups whole milk

1 cup condensed milk

2 cups water

1/2 tsp salt

1/2 tsp nutmeg

1 cup coconut milk

2 tbsp unsalted butter

1/4 cup granulated sugar

5 cinnamon sticks

2 tbsp vanilla extract

1/8 cup raisins (optional)

1 tsp whole all-spice

1/2 tsp cloves

Peel of one lime (optional)

# Caramelized Sweet Plantain

(Plátanos al caldero)

Preparation:

1. Peel the plantains and either leave them whole or cut them into three equal pieces. Lightly coat the pieces with granulated sugar. Cover and let them rest for 3 to 5 minutes to allow the sugar to slightly dissolve.

2. In a saucepan, combine the water, cloves, nutmeg, and cinnamon sticks. Bring the mixture to a boil, then remove from heat and set aside.

3. Heat the butter in a frying pan or skillet over medium heat. Once hot, fry the plantains, turning them every 1 to 2 minutes, until golden brown on all sides.

4. Carefully pour 1/3 cup of the prepared spice mixture, 1/4 cup of brown sugar, and salt over the golden plantains. Add 2 teaspoons of Dominican rum (optional). Reduce the heat and gently rotate the plantains until the sauce thickens into a syrup or reaches your desired consistency. The plantains should be served warm and drizzled with the syrup.

5. Serve and enjoy!

**Please note:** Alcohol is optional in this recipe and was included to reflect the original family recipe. If you choose to add it, please note that it may not be suitable for children. For family-friendly meals, I recommend omitting the alcohol to ensure the recipe is safe for all ages.

# Sweet Cornmeal Cake

(Arepa de maíz dulce)

Preparation:

1. In a saucepan, combine water, cloves, allspice, nutmeg, and cinnamon sticks. Bring the mixture to a boil and let it simmer for 7 to 10 minutes, then remove from heat.

2. Strain the mixture into a deep pot. Add whole milk, evaporated milk, coconut milk, vanilla extract, brown sugar, salt, and melted butter. Stir until well combined.

3. While stirring with a whisk to avoid lumps, gradually add the cornmeal. Return the pot to the stove over medium heat, stirring constantly. Cook until the mixture reaches a thick, paste-like consistency, then remove from heat.

4. Pour the mixture into a greased pan or round baking tray. Bake in a preheated oven at 350 °F (175 °C) for 45 to 50 minutes, or until the top is golden brown.

5. Allow the sweet cornmeal cake to cool, then remove it from the pan or tray.

6. Serve and enjoy!

2 cups fine cornmeal

2 cups whole milk

1 cup evaporated milk

4 tbsp unsalted butter

3 cups coconut milk

1 cup water

1/2 cup grinded coconut (optional)

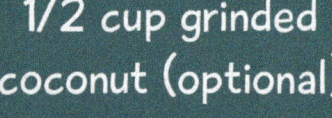
1 tsp vanilla extract

1/4 tsp salt

1/2 tsp cloves

1 tsp whole all-spice

1/2 cup raisins (optional)

1 1/2 cups brown sugar

5 cinnamon sticks

1/2 tsp nutmeg

# Flan

(Quesillo)

Preparation:

1. In a saucepan, combine water and sugar. Heat over medium heat, stirring until the sugar dissolves. Then increase the heat and cook until the sugar turns into a thick syrup.

2. Quickly but very carefully pour the syrup into the bottom and sides of a baking tray, and set it aside. Be cautious, as the syrup will be extremely hot.

3. In a blender, combine the eggs, condensed milk, evaporated milk, vanilla extract, salt, and Dominican rum (optional). Blend until well mixed.

4. Strain the mixture into a container, then pour it into the caramel-coated tray.

5. Place the tray in a bain-marie and bake in a preheated oven at 320 ºF (160ºC) for 45 to 50 minutes.

6. Allow the flan to cool to room temperature, then transfer it to the refrigerator and chill for 3 to 4 hours before serving.

7. Serve and enjoy!

**Please note:** Alcohol is optional in this recipe and was included to reflect the original family recipe. If you choose to add it, please note that it may not be suitable for children. For family- friendly meals, I recommend omitting the alcohol to ensure the recipe is safe for all ages.

4 eggs

1/8 tsp salt

1 can condensed milk (12 to 14 oz)

2 tbsp Dominican rum (optional)

1 can evaporated milk (12 to 14 oz)

2 tsp vanilla extract

## Caramel

1/16 salt (pinch)

2 tbsp water

1 cup granulated sugar

# Ingredients / Ingredientes

| English | Spanish |
|---|---|
| Oregano | Orégano |
| Thyme | Tomillo |
| Parsley | Perejil |
| Basil | Albahaca |
| Rosemary | Romero |
| Coriander | Culantro |
| Cilantro | Cilantro |
| Garlic | Ajo |
| Green onions | Cebolla verde |
| Cloves | Clavo dulce |
| Nutmeg | Nuez moscada |
| Whole all-spice | Malagueta |
| Cinnamon sticks | Palitos de canela |
| Black pepper | Pimienta negra |
| Lime peel | Cáscara de limon |
| Cubanelle pepper | Ají cubanela |
| Bell pepper | Pimiento morrón |
| Red onion | Cebolla roja |
| Celery | Apio |
| Plum tomatoes | Tomates barcelo |
| Cucumber | Pepino |
| Beefsteak tomato | Tomate de ensalada |
| Cabbage | Repollo |
| Beetroot | Remolacha |
| Romaine lettuce | Lechuga romana |
| Rice | Arroz |
| Coconut milk | Leche de coco |
| Unsalted butter | Mantequilla sin sal |
| Butter | Mantequilla |

# Ingredients / Ingredientes

| English | Spanish |
|---|---|
| Cornmeal | Harina de maíz |
| Green plantains | Plátanos verdes |
| Sweet plantains | Plátanos maduros |
| Salt | Sal |
| Sugar (unspecified) | Azúcar |
| White sugar | Azúcar blanca |
| Brown sugar | Azúcar morena |
| Granulated sugar | Azúcar granulada |
| Vinegar | Vinagre |
| Balsamic vinegar | Vinagre balsámico |
| Olive oil | Aceite de oliva |
| Honey | Miel |
| Agave | Jarabe de agave |
| Tomato paste | Pasta de tomate |
| Cup ketchup | Taza de kétchup |
| Chicken | Pollo |
| Salami | Salami |
| Eggs | Huevos |
| Red beans | Frijoles rojos |
| Chicken bouillon | Caldo de pollo |
| Whole milk | Leche entera |
| Evaporated milk | Leche evaporada |
| Condensed milk | Leche condensada |
| Raisins | Pasas |
| Sour oranges | Naranjas agrias |
| Vanilla extract | Extracto de vainilla |

## About the Author

Enmerlin has deep roots in the Dominican Republic, where she spent her childhood surrounded by the love and guidance of her grandparents, Dilia and Carmito.

Growing up in this rich cultural environment, Enmerlin was also closely connected to her aunts and uncles, who played important roles in shaping her values and passions. Her upbringing in a close-knit family and community laid the foundation for her deep appreciation of tradition, family bonds, and the significance of sharing meaningful experiences.

Inspired by the history and gastronomy of her homeland, Enmerlin draws much of her creativity from the vibrant flavors, ingredients, and culinary customs of the Dominican Republic. Her passion for cooking and its cultural importance shines through in this book. She believes that food has the power to bring people together, nurture relationships, and preserve memories, which is why she hopes her book encourages families of all kinds to embrace cooking and share meals as a way to connect with one another.

This book marks a significant milestone in Enmerlin's writing journey, as it is her first published work. She plans to continue writing and share more stories and insights with her readers in the future. Through her work, Enmerlin hopes to inspire others to explore the richness of their heritage, celebrate family, and create lasting traditions centered around food and togetherness.

## About the Illustrator

Mousam Banerjee is a full-time artist and illustrator who loves to remain engaged in painting everything from whimsical children's books to realistic concept art. Born into an artistic family, he was keen on creating original paintings right from childhood. With a post graduate diploma in Fine Arts, he has now made a career in Digital illustrations.

You can reach out to him at www.illus-station.com or on instagram at illusstation.kids

www.ingramcontent.com/pod-product-compliance
Lightning Source LLC
Chambersburg PA
CBHW051328110526
44582CB00003B/80